Mariam Al-Ijliya

The Astrolabe Designer

Author

Rafia Rehman

Illustrator

Muhammad Yousaf Rana

Additional Contributors

Dr. Abdul Rehman
Umair Zia

In Collaboration with

Habib ur Rehman Research Foundation

And

Knowledge is a Treasure

That will follow you everywhere

Chinese proverb

4th century A.H. (10th century A.D.)

The illustrations of Mariam Al-Ijliya in this book are based on the artist's imagination on how she may have looked like.

It was a cold Saturday afternoon in late November. The six friends: Heba, Ezzah, Kabens, Melaclap, Janeed and Saya, decided to meet again in the town park where they had found the treasure chest few weeks earlier.

Weather was starting to get cold. The children decided to move the chest to Ezzah's home after that day so they could continue to meet and learn during the snowy winter months.

They dug up the chest from behind the big oak tree, where they have previously hidden it, covered with dirt and leaves.

As they opened the chest to take the 'Book of Jewels' out, a strange circular thing fell. Ezzah extended her hand and caught it. The object was gold in color, and made out of metal. Different numbers and letters were engraved on it. There was also a pointer similar to the hand of a clock connected in the center.

Suddenly, Heba remembered that she had seen a picture of a similar looking object in one of the pages of the book.

The children sat in a circle and placed the book in the middle. Heba opened the book to the page about the circular object. With a smile on her face and an expression of curiosity, Heba read the title of the picture; "Astrolabe".

"What's an Astrolabe?" questioned Kabens.

The page next to the picture of the Astrolabe had a map.

Janeed loved geography, so he took the book and started to read the map.

"Here is the park," Janeed said, and continued, "the big oak tree is right here," Janeed pointed at the circle shaped like a tree, "following the dots, it takes us across the street to this building marked with an 'X'".

"I think its the library," exclaimed Kabens.

"That's correct! The map is taking us to the Library," confirmed Janeed.

As everyone started to get up, a sudden breeze caused the page to turn revealing another map. It was the map of inside the library giving instructions to go to a hidden room.

The children took the book and started to walk towards the library. Once inside, they used the second map to guide them to the secret room. It was located near the children's book section behind an old wooden bookshelf.

All of them had been to the library many times before,

but had never noticed this door.

After mustering up some courage they opened the door.

Heba, Ezzah, and

Janeed decided to

go in first.

As they entered the

room, their attire

changed.

The room was lit bright. Sunshine came in through the window on one of the walls with green curtains pulled back.

In the center of the room, on a wooden bench, a young lady was sitting and working on a gold colored circular device. The device looked very similar to the picture of the Astrolabe that the children had found in the book earlier.

Heba, Ezzah, and Janeed slowly moved closer to the table. Kabens, Saya, and Melaclap followed into the room as well.

The lady raised her head, looked at the children with a smile and greeted them.

"Welcome my dear children," she said, "I have been waiting for you. It seems that you have stumbled upon the page about the Astrolabe in the Book of Jewels".

Children were startled to hear that and looked at each other in awe.

"Yes, that's correct," Melaclap remarked.

"We found a map in the book that has led us to this room," added Heba.

With politeness the children introduced themselves one at a time, and then asked the lady to tell them about her.

The lady stood up, and asked the children to sit on a large wooden bench. She then started to tell about herself. "My name is Mariam Al-Ijliya, but everyone remembers me from my title 'Al-Astrolabia', which means 'the Astrolabe maker'. It is because I spent a lot of time designing, making and perfecting Astrolabes, which is actually this device that I am working on right now, and what you found in your book."

Mariam paused to show the device she was making and then continued .

"I was born into a family of engineers during the mid fourth century A.H. (tenth century A.D.), in the city of Aleppo, which is located in the modern day northern Syria."

"I always had a keen interest in reading and learning about different topics. As I grew older, my interests ultimately led me to study astronomy, something not many girls were interested in during my time. With much hard work I ultimately became an Astronomer."

Mariam continued to tell about herself.

"While growing up, I would occasionally observe my father constructing various tools and instruments. One item that he used to make often was the Astrolabe. For a period of time my father worked for Netulus, who was an instrument maker famous for making some of the best Astrolabes. In fact, today the oldest surviving Astrolabe in the world is the one made by Netulus."

"I was always fascinated by my father's work and would sometimes assist him in his shop. By observing, and helping my father, I soon started to make my own Astrolabes."

"Using my imagination, creativity and applying my knowledge of Astronomy, I came up with a new design of the Astrolabe which was superior, and more precise than any other available at that time."

The children were listening attentively. Ezzah decided to ask the question that was on everyone's mind.

"You mentioned the word 'Astrolabe' many times. Can you please tell us more about it?"

"Absolutely!" replied Mariam, and continued, "an Astrolabe is a scientific instrument that has multiple uses."

"Primarily it was a tool used by the astronomers for the measurements of stars and planets. It was also used to estimate time, similar to a clock, and to calculate direction, like a compass."

"Think of the Astrolabe as a smart phone that the astronomers and scientists used hundreds of years ago for a range of complex calculations and measurements."

"Wow, that's amazing," remarked Saya.

Mariam continued to tell more about the Astrolabe.

"Although the Astrolabe was used all over the world, it was an especially important instrument for the Muslims. They used it to help them to accurately calculate the direction of the Kaaba from anywhere in the world, estimate the times for the five daily prayers, as well as to determine the start of the lunar calendar months."

Mariam continued, "The Astrolabe design that I made was a significant improvement over the ones that were made by others. Their uniqueness got the attention of Sayf Al-Dawla, who was the ruler of the city of Aleppo. He gave me a job at his office to make Astrolabes for everyone to use. Imagine the president giving you a job because you are the best at what you do. My Astrolabes became the basis of the modern day's communication and navigation systems."

It was the first time the children had learned about the Astrolabe. They were curious to know more about it.

"Let me take you on a short journey and demonstrate how to use the Astrolabe," Mariam said.

Children got excited as they wanted to learn how to use the instrument. They got up and followed Mariam. As they walked out the back door, to their surprise, they were no longer in their town. It was also dark outside. The sky was filled with stars.

Mariam first explained the details of each of the measurements and charts on the instrument, and then lifted the Astrolabe demonstrating how to use it to locate the position of different objects with respect to the horizon.

Palomar
Observatory
California
Institue of Technology

They first observed the moon, then the planet Jupiter, and lastly the brightest star in the sky known as Sirius.

After demonstrating the Astrolabe, Mariam allowed everyone to take turns. It was a complex device to understand and use, but the children were happy that they were able to begin their learnings about it from one of the best makers of the Astrolabe.

"Did you know why I brought you outside of the Palomar Observatory?" questioned Mariam.

The children remained silent, curious to know the answer.

Mariam explained, "Its because my work was honored by them when in 1990 at this observatory a main-belt asteroid 7060 was discovered and named after me, 'Al-'Ijliya."

Children were flabbergasted to hear that.

After completing the tour they came back to the library. It was now time for them to return home. They thanked Mariam and promised that they will continue to learn more about her and the instrument that she used to make.

Snow season was approaching. As agreed earlier the children moved the chest along with the 'Book of Jewels' to Ezzah's home. They decided to meet during the winter break to learn about another personality.

Mariam Al-Ijliya

The Astrolabe Designer

ACTIVITIES

WORD SEARCH

Y	L	Y	M	L	Y	K	J	E	M	A	R	I	A	M
N	Z	V	E	C	E	I	B	F	A	V	M	G	R	C
M	B	I	A	Y	N	A	O	L	L	J	M	G	R	Z
H	A	C	S	S	L	S	E	G	U	P	Y	Z	G	X
K	F	B	U	O	T	P	I	P	I	M	T	G	C	S
K	T	I	R	O	P	E	I	R	O	P	B	Z	O	M
A	F	T	E	O	O	T	N	N	I	N	D	W	Y	L
M	S	D	M	J	E	N	O	A	X	U	P	B	Q	F
A	J	F	E	R	P	R	F	O	L	Z	S	M	Y	G
F	X	O	N	B	T	J	L	T	S	P	A	I	U	H
S	L	H	T	S	B	J	T	Z	R	G	D	Y	D	L
M	Y	Q	A	O	B	S	E	R	V	A	T	O	R	Y
A	A	N	V	D	I	K	K	V	D	D	Q	Z	O	W
R	A	N	D	Q	K	Z	R	B	W	E	K	Q	A	X
R	R	Z	N	O	I	T	A	G	I	V	A	N	U	O

MARIAM

ALEPPO

ASTROLABE

ASTRONOMY

JUPITER

MEASUREMENT

NAVIGATION

OBSERVATORY

PLANETS

SIRIUS

Connect the Dots

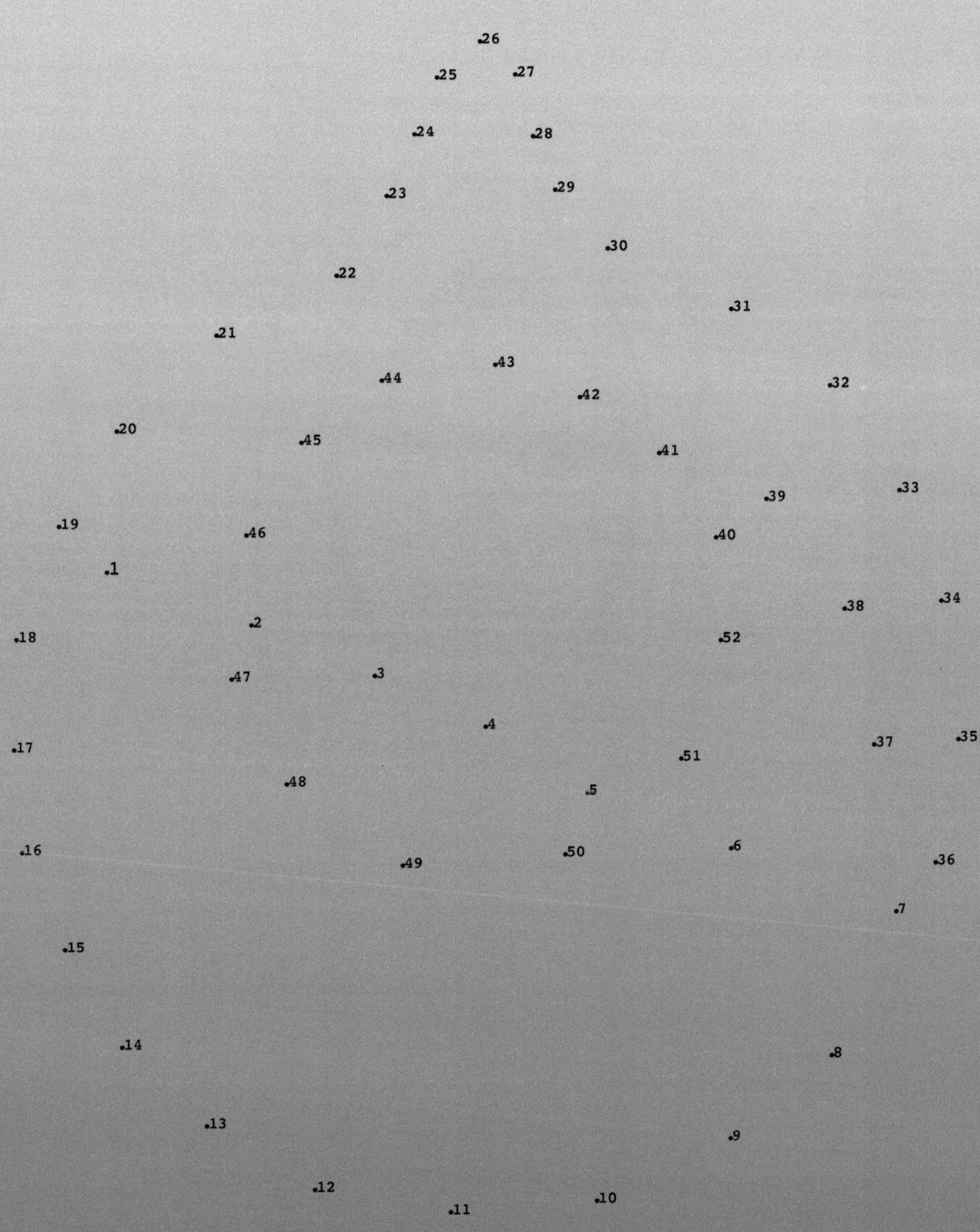

Palomar
Observatory
California
Institue of Technology

About the Series:

Nurturing courage, confidence and love of knowledge in young minds through stories on great individuals and leaders that transformed the world through their wisdom, inventions, discoveries and exploration.

Like, Share, Follow us on:

Instagram

www.instagram.com/pioneerbookseries

Facebook

www.facebook.com/pioneerbookseries

Youtube Channel

Pioneer Book Series for Kids

About the Author and Contributors:

Rafia Rehman, a mother of two has a Masters degree in Clinical Mental Health Counseling. She has worked at various agencies in United States of America and Pakistan providing mental health services to a diverse group of individuals including children. She is passionate about the concept of holistic education.

Dr. Abdul Rehman is a renowned Architect and a life long educator. He received his Ph.D in Architecture from the Ion Minco Institute of Architecture in Bucharest, Romania. He served as a professor and the Director of School of Architecture at the University of Engineering and Technology in Lahore, Pakistan. He has been a fellow at Dumbarton Oaks, Harvard University, and Massachusetts Institute of Technology, and has authored numerous books and publications. (www.drabdulrehman.com)

Umair Zia holds degrees in Electrical, and Systems Engineering and a graduate certificate in Mechanical Engineering. Serving a career in the Electric Power industry he held numerous technical and leadership positions. He has also served on the boards of non-profits, and as a teacher and Vice President of curriculum development at Al-Itqaan school in Worcester, MA.

About the Illustrator:

Muhammad Yousaf Rana is a career artist, caricaturist and illustrator. He has taught the art of caricature and illustration as well as conducted workshops at several institutions including the Oriental College of Arts and the University of The Punjab. He has a vast experience of illustrating children's books.